Growth

Feeding and respiration make cells become larger as the cell material builds up. When a normal cell has grown enough, it divides and becomes two cells. The two cells then grow by producing more cell material. An organism continues to grow as its cells grow.

Sensitivity

Organisms are affected by their surrounding conditions, such as the presence of sunlight or chemicals. These things are called **stimuli**. Organisms need to detect, or be sensitive to stimuli in order to respond to them.

Reproduction

The process of creating a new organism from either one or two parents is called reproduction. With two parents this is called **sexual** reproduction. With one parent, it is called **asexual** reproduction.

Locomotion

All organisms are capable of movement, or locomotion. An animal can move its whole body, but plants only move parts of themselves, towards or away from stimuli.

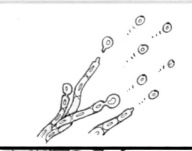

Death

Organisms eventually cease to perform any life functions. This condition is called death.

SUMMARY

There are many different species of organisms. Living organisms have characteristics and functions in common.

Death occurs when all the life functions of an organism end.

NON-LIFE

Living, dead, extinct and non-living things

It is not always easy to tell whether an organism or other object is alive or dead. For example, a **virus** is a tiny package of chemicals which sometimes seems to be living. However, a virus is not a cell, and stays inactive unless it can get into a living cell. It can only reproduce by hijacking some of the building material of a living cell.

Some living organisms are inactive, or **dormant**, between periods of activity. For example, some trees appear to die in winter and come back to life in spring. Some organisms, such as fungi and bacteria, are able to produce tiny, seed-like **spores** or **cysts**. These are tiny packets of living material which stay dormant until conditions become more favourable for life processes.

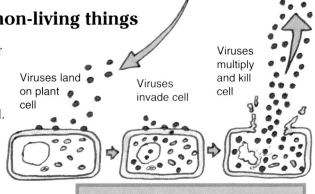

Plant virus

Viruses escape

Viruses land on plant cell

Viruses invade cell

Viruses multiply and kill cell

What characteristics of organisms do viruses not possess?

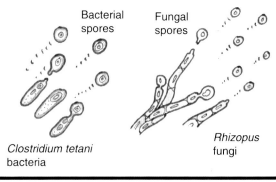

Bacterial spores

Fungal spores

Clostridium tetani bacteria

Rhizopus fungi

Sterile jar of damp bread crumbs

Sterile jars

Sterilizer

Mouldy bread

Notepad

Investigation

Using this equipment, how could you show that fungi spores can be dormant for long periods of time?

How could you be sure that a jar is free of spores to start with?

How could you show that spores are able to become active again?

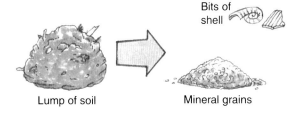

Lump of soil

Mineral grains

Bits of shell

Pebbles

Plant material

Bacteria and fungi

Dead insects

Bone

A living organism is made up of **organic** materials which always contain carbon. When an organism dies, its remains are dead organic material. **Inorganic** material has never been alive. Soil is made up of organic material and inorganic material.

Is a bone organic or inorganic?

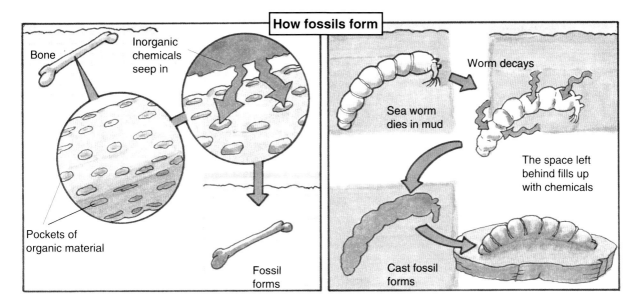

How fossils form

Bone

Inorganic chemicals seep in

Pockets of organic material

Fossil forms

Sea worm dies in mud

Worm decays

The space left behind fills up with chemicals

Cast fossil forms

Bones and shells are mostly hard inorganic material, but contain small pockets of organic material. When an organism dies most of its organic material is usually eaten up, or made to **decay**, by small living organisms such as bacteria. All the pockets of organic material in bones and shells disappear. Inorganic chemicals may then seep into the small spaces left. Eventually, the bone or shell becomes an inorganic, solid **fossil**. Most fossils are more than 10,000 years old.

A soft organism, such as a leaf or a sponge, is organic material all the way through. It is likely to decay without leaving a trace. Sometimes, however, a soft organism decays very slowly in mud, and inorganic chemicals may seep into the space left behind. A solid outline, or **cast** of the organism forms and becomes a fossil. **Fossil fuels** are the carbon-based remains of dead plants and animals which were not decayed by other organisms.

Some famous extinctions

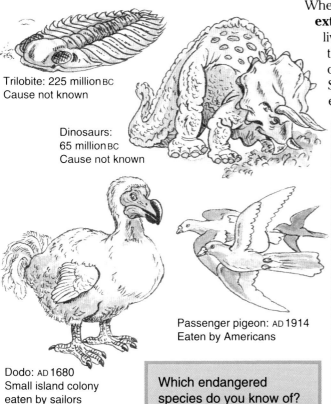

Trilobite: 225 million BC
Cause not known

Dinosaurs:
65 million BC
Cause not known

Passenger pigeon: AD 1914
Eaten by Americans

Dodo: AD 1680
Small island colony eaten by sailors

When a species of organisms dies, the species is **extinct**. For example, many species of trilobite lived between 600 and 225 million years ago, then they all became extinct. Other species of organisms became extinct more recently. Species which are in danger of becoming extinct are called **endangered species**.

Which endangered species do you know of?

SUMMARY

Viruses are non-living things which have some of the characteristics of living organisms.

Some organisms may be dormant when conditions are not suitable for active life.

All materials are either organic or inorganic, or a mixture of both.

Fossils are the inorganic remains or casts of dead plants and animals.

Fossil fuels are the organic remains of dead plants and animals.

A species is extinct when all of its members are dead.

THE VARIETY OF LIFE

How organisms are classified

Plants and animals are often known by different names in different parts of a country. For example, the crane fly and the harvestman are both called 'Daddy long-legs'. The dandelion has about thirty other English names. Around the world, there are thousands of different languages, each with their own names for plants and animals. To avoid confusion over which creatures are being discussed, biologists use agreed Latin names for organisms.

Crane fly

Harvestman

Dandelion

The Swedish botanist Carolus Linnaeus (1707–78) developed the idea of classifying organisms and giving them Latin names.

Common names for organisms, such as Daddy long-legs, often point out some visible feature of an organism. However, the crane fly and the harvestman both have long legs, so this is not a clear enough description of either organism.

Can you name any other animals with long legs?

What differences can you see between the crane fly and the harvestman?

What differences are there between crane flies and house flies?

Biologists ask and answer a series of **key** questions about an organism so they can identify and classify it. Linnaeus also classified organisms according to their visible features. Today we use more detailed methods, such as looking at the cells of an organism. However, there are still different opinions on the correct way to classify many organisms.

Linnaeus' system of classification gave each organism first a group name, or **genus**, and then an individual describing name. The two names together describe a **species**. For example, all domestic dogs are of the species *Canis familiaris*. Canis is Latin for the dog genus, and *familiaris* is Latin for 'friendly' or 'domesticated'. There are many other species of dog-like animals, such as the wolf (*Canis lupus*, or wolf dog) and the coyote (*Canis latris*, or barking dog).

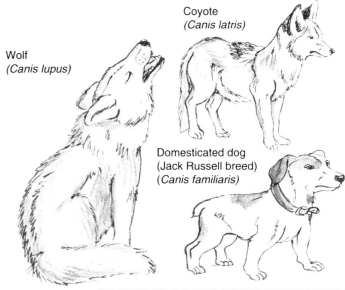

Coyote
(*Canis latris*)

Wolf
(*Canis lupus*)

Domesticated dog
(Jack Russell breed)
(*Canis familiaris*)

There are about 300 breeds of *Canis familiaris*. Why do you think they are not all given different species names?

Organisms of a species can normally breed with each other, but cannot normally breed with other species. This means that even the most different-looking domestic dogs can mate and have puppies, but coyotes and wolves cannot.

Some animals, such as the fox, are dog-like but are too different from wolves or domestic dogs to be included in the same genus. Foxes are classified in the genus *Vulpes*. All dog-like animals are grouped together in a **family**, called the Canidae. The Canidae are all meat-eaters, so they can be placed in a larger group containing the other families of meat-eaters, such as cats (Felidae).

A group of families is called an **order**. The order of meat-eaters is the Carnivora. The Carnivora are in turn members of an even larger group, or **class**, of animals which suckle their young. This class is the mammals, or Mammalia. Mammals have backbones, so they are put into a yet larger group, or **phylum** (plural phyla) of animals with backbones. The phylum of animals with backbones is called the Chordata and includes snakes and birds.

Human classification

Species: *Homo sapiens*

Genus: *Homo*

Family: Hominid

Sub-order: Anthropoid

Order: Primate

Class: Mammal

Phylum: Chordata

Kingdom: Animal

All animals are members of the **animal kingdom**, or Animalia. There are five kingdoms of life on Earth:

Monerans: single-celled bacteria with no nucleus

Example: *Lactobacillus bulgaricus*

Protistans: single-celled organisms with a nucleus

Example: Amoeba

Green Plants: multi-celled plants which photosynthesize

Example: Daisy

Fungi: multi-celled plants which do not photosynthesize

Example: Mushroom

Animals: multi-celled organisms which cannot make their own food

Example: Cow

What class of animals do you think a cow is in?

SUMMARY

Organisms are given agreed Latin names to ensure their correct identification.

Organisms are classified by answering key questions about their physical features and comparing them with other organisms. Biologists differ as to the correct classification of some organisms.

Members of a species can interbreed, but cannot normally breed with members of other species.

There are five kingdoms of life on Earth. Each kingdom can be subdivided into phylum, class, order, family, genus and species.

NATURAL SELECTION
Evolution and the survival of the fittest

Linnaeus thought that all species had always stayed the same. Later biologists realized that species may die out or change. Fossil records show that the first organisms were small and primitive but later organisms were often larger and more complex. For example, 3 billion years ago, the most complex organisms were similar to modern bacteria. About 600 million years ago, the more complex trilobites had come into existence. Dinosaurs appeared about 225 million years ago. Modern humans appeared about 80,000 years ago. Several theories were put forward as to how this development process, or **evolution**, worked. Charles Darwin first introduced the idea of **natural selection** of species to explain evolution.

When members of a species reproduce, the offspring usually have similar body shapes to their parent or parents. For example, male and female elephants mate and produce more elephants. The reproductive cells of organisms contain **genes** which pass on the parents' characteristics to the offspring. Once in a while, the offspring is different because a **mutation** has happened. A mutation happens when the parent genes are altered or damaged. Genes can be damaged by viruses or radiation. Mutations can be fatal or helpful, or may make no difference to the survival chances of the new organism.

The English naturalist Charles Robert Darwin (1809–1882) outlined the mechanism for evolutionary change in his book called *On the Origin of Species by Means of Natural Selection, or the Preservation of Favoured Races in the Struggle for Life.*

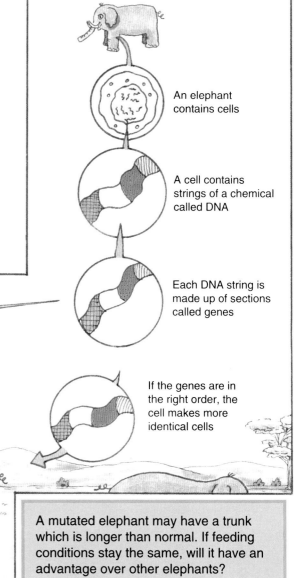

An elephant contains cells

A cell contains strings of a chemical called DNA

Each DNA string is made up of sections called genes

If the genes are in the wrong order, the cell makes more mutated cells

If the genes are in the right order, the cell makes more identical cells

Mutated elephant

Normal elephant

A mutated elephant may have a trunk which is longer than normal. If feeding conditions stay the same, will it have an advantage over other elephants?

Organisms depend on their environment for food, warmth, air and shelter. An organism which does not get these things may die before it can reproduce. An organism which does get the things it needs is likely to survive long enough to reproduce.

If there is a shortage of food on the ground, will the long-trunked elephant have an advantage over the others?

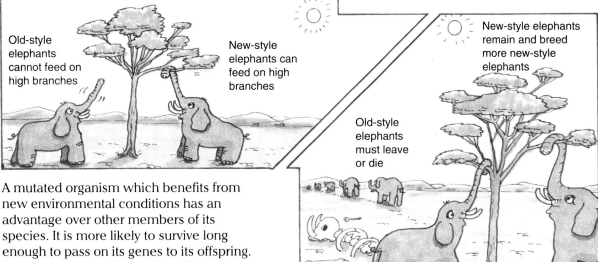

Old-style elephants cannot feed on high branches

New-style elephants can feed on high branches

New-style elephants remain and breed more new-style elephants

Old-style elephants must leave or die

A mutated organism which benefits from new environmental conditions has an advantage over other members of its species. It is more likely to survive long enough to pass on its genes to its offspring. A new group, or **sub-species**, of organism may then appear. A sub-species can usually mate with members of the original species and produce more of the new sub-species. Given enough time, the new sub-species may evolve into a new species. The original species may die out or move away.

What may happen to the new species of long-trunked elephant if tree trunks begin to grow much taller?

An organism's environment changes as the organism's behaviour changes. For example, a type of tree might also evolve into a longer-trunked species, preventing its branches being eaten by elephants. This may also affect other organisms such as the ants or squirrels which live in trees. These animals might in turn die out or evolve. Over millions of years, all organisms on Earth are likely to gradually change as they **adapt** to new conditions.

Coelacanth

The coelacanth is a species of fish which has not died out or changed much over the last 60 million years. Why do you think this is so?

Taller tree species evolves

Now the new-style elephants can no longer feed

SUMMARY

Species become extinct, or change over long periods of time by a process called evolution.

Mutation and natural selection are the mechanisms of evolution.

Organisms which are fit to survive will pass on their genes to their offspring.

Species evolve as they adapt to environmental changes over long periods of time.

HABITATS

Organisms are adapted to where they live

The place where an organism usually lives is called its **habitat**. All of the billions of habitats on Earth is called the **biosphere**. A habitat is usually home for a **community** of organisms. For example, a pond habitat has a community of organisms such as pond weeds, ducks, fish, insects and bacteria.

A habitat may have many parts which are linked to each other. For example, the mud in a pond is wet because of the water above it. Most pond weeds need mud to grow in. A duck needs water to float on.

Fish eggs on pond weed

A litre of pond mud may contain billions of bacteria and other tiny organisms

Each organism in a community relates to its neighbours and its habitat in different ways. An organism is said to occupy a **niche** in a community. For example, a duck's niche may be to eat pond weed. A fish may eat insects in the water and lay eggs on the pond weed. Bacteria may eat dead organisms in the mud.

Why do fish continue to live under water if there are more insects above the surface?

Successful organisms are adapted to their niche. For example, most fish cannot breathe air but get the oxygen they need from the water. Fish eggs have to be laid in water for them to hatch. As long as nothing happens to the pond and there are plenty of underwater insects, pond fish species are likely to survive.

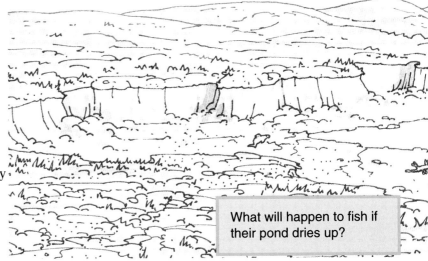

What will happen to fish if their pond dries up?

The organisms in a community depend on the various features of their habitat. If food gathering becomes difficult, some organisms may be able to find a similar habitat elsewhere. Other organisms may not be able to leave. If a food resource on which several organisms or species depend becomes scarce, then the organisms are in **competition** for that food. If one species is successful at the expense of another, it is known as a **dominant** species.

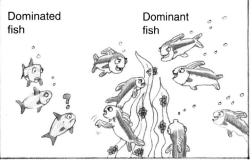

Dominated fish

Dominant fish

Flying fish

Climbing perch

Organisms can either die, move away or adapt. The African perch has adapted to its changing evironment by learning to climb trees and rocks in search of scarce food. Flying fish can glide through the air to avoid being caught by other fish. Archer-fish spit at flying insects to make them fall in the water.

Archer-fish

An organism may die if an important feature of its habitat disappears. A sudden, deadly change in a habitat is called a **catastrophe**. Organisms do not have time to adapt or escape when a catastrophe happens. A catastrophe which destroys all examples of a particular habitat may make some species extinct. When a catastrophe seriously affects the biosphere, many different habitats may be destroyed, and **mass extinctions** may occur.

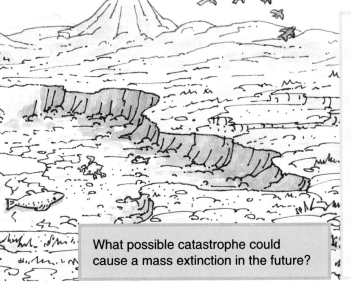

What possible catastrophe could cause a mass extinction in the future?

SUMMARY

The place where an organism usually lives is called its habitat.

A habitat contains a community of species which are adapted to their environment.

Each species occupies a niche in its habitat.

An organism may be in competition with other organisms in the same niche.

A sudden, deadly change in a habitat or in the biosphere is called a catastrophe. It may result in species extinctions.

TIME AND TIDE

Adapting to repeated changes in the environment

Organisms are adapted to the regular, predictable changes which occur in many habitats. For example, daylight and darkness occur on a daily basis. Animals which are most active in daylight are called **diurnal** animals. Those most active at night are called **nocturnal** animals. Nocturnal animals are adapted to seeking food when there is little light.

In what ways do you think these animals are adapted to a nocturnal life?

Bush baby

Shrew

Pit viper

Heat from prey

Adaptations may include big eyes which trap more light than small ones, or very sensitive noses for sniffing out food in the dark. Some snakes can even sense the heat given off by their animal food as it hides in the dark.

A nocturnal animal usually sleeps in a sheltered spot, such as under a rock, during the day. A diurnal animal tends to sleep somewhere safe at night. Plants feed during the day because they depend on sunlight for their energy. During the night, many species of plants close their petals or fold their leaves. This is to stop unwanted insects entering the flower, or to save moisture or to protect the plant from the cold.

Oxalis flowers open in sunlight

Oxalis flowers close in shade

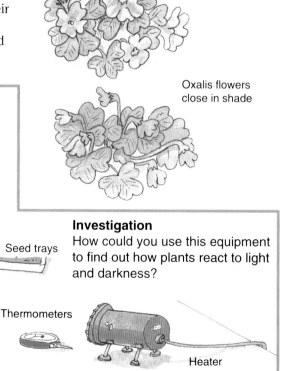

Permanent lighting

Water

Seed trays

Black polythene sheets

Quick-growing seedlings

Thermometers

Heater

Investigation
How could you use this equipment to find out how plants react to light and darkness?

Many organisms not only respond to regular stimuli, but can also sense the passage of time. For example, a plant placed in artificial light may continue to open and close its petals in time with the daily periods of light and darkness it would normally experience. It is said to have an 'internal clock' or **biorhythm** which regulates its behaviour and bodily functions. Most organisms have biorhythms. People who go on long flights may feel unwell if their biorhythm clock does not match the real local time. This problem is called **jet lag**.

Could plants suffer from jet lag?

Some coastal organisms are adapted to tidal changes. For example, some tidal mud dwellers breathe air. At low tide they fill their tiny burrows with a bubble of air. This lasts them for the next six hours while the high tide covers the burrow with water.

Spring

Summer

Autumn

Winter

Biorhythms are also responsible for seasonal adaptations. Many plants have a yearly cycle of growth and dormancy. This cycle is not necessarily caused directly by changes in sunlight or temperature. For example, daffodils may be damaged if they come up when there is still snow on the ground. Despite the cold weather, daffodils still follow their biorhythm clock and come up anyway. This is because on average each year it tells them the right time to start growing.

Animals are also affected by seasonal environmental changes. Some animals sleep during the winter, or **hibernate**. Others sleep during the summer, or **estivate**. Others grow thicker, thinner or differently coloured fur during different parts of the year. Some animals move or **migrate** to a more comfortable habitat for some of the year. All of these adaptations help animals to survive repeated habitat changes.

How might a tree's seasonal changes affect animals which depend on it?

Why might some animals sleep in the winter and others sleep in the summer?

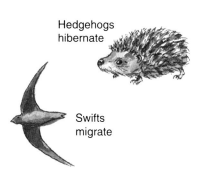

Hedgehogs hibernate

Swifts migrate

Lungfish estivate

SUMMARY
Organisms are adapted to repeated, predictable changes in their environments.

Adaptations to repeated environmental changes are often programmed by biorhythms.

Biorhythms can trigger changes of both body form and behaviour.

BODY FORM

Shape, function and the environment

The body form, or **physical adaptation**, of an organism is related to the conditions in its habitat. For example, animals which live in cold places need a warm coat of fur, feathers or fat.

Arctic tern

Polar bear

Walrus

Most animals need to be able to move in order to feed or mate. The body shape of an organism is related to how it moves in its habitat. For example, walkers have legs, swimmers are usually streamlined and fliers have wings.

> How do each of these three animals protect themselves from the cold?
>
> How do the body shapes of these animals differ?

The body shape is also related to the food an organism needs. For example, most plants have roots for drawing in nutrients and water from soil, and leaves for drawing in air. In deserts there may be no soil, so some rootless plants draw in water through their leaves. Other desert plants, such as cacti, have roots and fat spiny leaves for storing water over long periods.

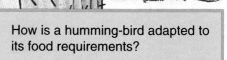

> How is a humming-bird adapted to its food requirements?

Once an animal has found food, it has to be able to eat it. For example, humming birds have long beaks for sipping nectar from flowers. Parrots have heavy beaks for cracking nuts. Meat-eating animals, or **carnivores**, need pointed teeth for tearing meat. Vegetarian animals, or **herbivores**, need sharp front teeth for cutting through plant material and grinding back teeth for chewing it. **Omnivores** eat both meat and plants.

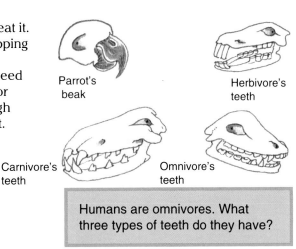

Parrot's beak

Herbivore's teeth

Carnivore's teeth

Omnivore's teeth

Humans are omnivores. What three types of teeth do they have?

Suggest a physiological reason why trees and squirrels move at different speeds.

An organism's physical adaptations are usually visible. Less visible adaptations such as chemical or microscopic make-up are called **physiological adaptations**. For example, mammals can control their body temperature by internal chemical means, but reptiles cannot. Mammals and reptiles are physiologically different. Animal cells and plant cells are also physiologically different.

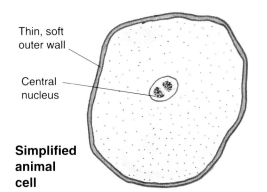

Thin, soft outer wall

Central nucleus

Simplified animal cell

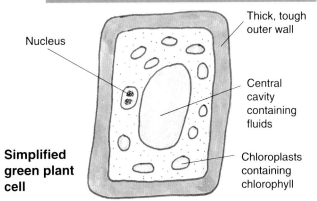

Nucleus

Thick, tough outer wall

Central cavity containing fluids

Chloroplasts containing chlorophyll

Simplified green plant cell

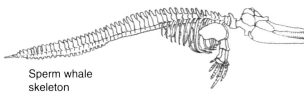

Blue whale skeleton

Sperm whale skeleton

What differences are there between these two skeletons?

What other swimmers do you know of which evolved from walkers or fliers?

The body shape of organisms may evolve over long periods of time in response to environmental changes. For example, it is thought that sperm whales evolved from four-legged carnivores which hunted coastal animals about 50 million years ago. Sperm whales gradually became adapted to a swimming life. Their legs disappeared and their bodies became more streamlined. Blue whales probably evolved from coastal herbivores.

SUMMARY
The body shape of an organism is usually determined by its environment and behaviour.
Physical adaptations are usually visible.
Physiological adaptations are microscopic or chemical.
The body shapes of organisms gradually evolve in response to environmental changes.

SURVIVAL

How organisms protect themselves from others

Organisms need to be able to **defend** themselves from other species and from members of their own species. All organisms have their own ways of defending themselves.

When do you think organisms have to defend themselves from members of their own species?

What weapons are being used by these stags?

A few male animals regularly **fight** other males of their species for the chance to mate with the females of a group. This usually means that the strongest male passes on his genes. Some females may also fight for mating rights, but more often fight to protect their young.

Rutting stags

For its own defence, an organism may use active weapons such as antlers, horns, claws, teeth and venom. An organism may also use passive weapons such as thorns, spines or poison. Organisms may also make threatening gestures. Poisonous organisms are often very brightly coloured to show their enemies that they are not safe to eat. The flavours of herbs may make these plants distasteful to herbivores.

Cat making threatening gestures

Holly

Very few animals kill members of their own species in fights. The losers tend to retreat after a fight or threat of a fight. Threats from other species are usually much more dangerous, and threatened organisms may have to **flee** from these. Many animals run, fly, swim or wriggle away from a threat. Plants cannot move bodily, but may still be able to avoid danger. For example, some plants have sensitive hairs on their leaves which tell the leaf to curl away from things which touch them.

Tarragon

Ladybird

How do these organisms defend themselves?

Birds can fly away from danger

Mimosa pudica

Worms can wriggle to safety very quickly

Organisms may actively **hide** from danger. Some sand lizards can burrow quickly into the sand to gain safety. Other organisms may take shelter under rocks. A tortoise carries its shelter with it. Plants cannot hide so well as animals because they need stay in the open to receive sunlight.

Sand lizards can hide in sand

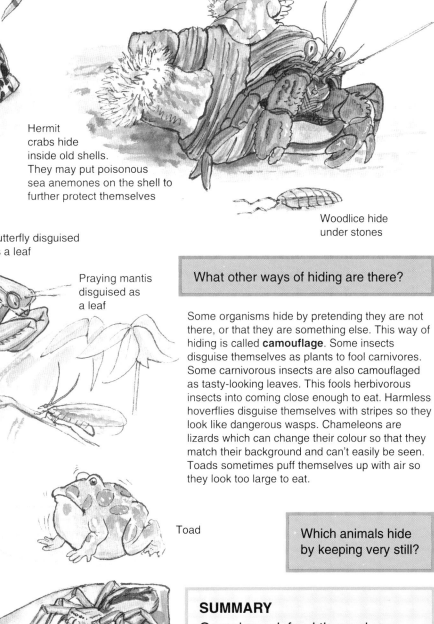

Tortoise hiding in its shell

Hermit crabs hide inside old shells. They may put poisonous sea anemones on the shell to further protect themselves

Woodlice hide under stones

Butterfly disguised as a leaf

Praying mantis disguised as a leaf

Hoverfly

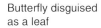

Toad

What other ways of hiding are there?

Some organisms hide by pretending they are not there, or that they are something else. This way of hiding is called **camouflage**. Some insects disguise themselves as plants to fool carnivores. Some carnivorous insects are also camouflaged as tasty-looking leaves. This fools herbivorous insects into coming close enough to eat. Harmless hoverflies disguise themselves with stripes so they look like dangerous wasps. Chameleons are lizards which can change their colour so that they match their background and can't easily be seen. Toads sometimes puff themselves up with air so they look too large to eat.

Which animals hide by keeping very still?

Some hungry female spiders eat the smaller male as soon as they have mated. To protect themselves, some male spiders bring the female a gift of an insect he has caught and wrapped in silk. This is to **bribe** the female so that he can mate safely while she is eating something else.

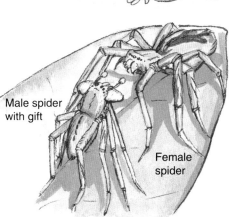

Male spider with gift

Female spider

SUMMARY
Organisms defend themselves actively or passively.

Very few organisms fight to kill members of their own species.

Organisms defend themselves by fighting, fleeing, hiding, using camouflage and giving gifts.

PREDATOR AND PREY

Feeding relationships between organisms

Green plants take in water, carbon dioxide and soil chemicals. They use the energy from sunlight to turn these things into food. Plants also produce food for animals. Unlike plants, animals cannot produce their food from inorganic materials. Herbivores are called **primary consumers** because they eat plants. Carnivores eat herbivores so they are called **secondary consumers**. Carnivores which eat other carnivores are called **tertiary consumers**. Omnivores can eat either plants or animals. A simple sequence of eating and being eaten is called a **food chain**.

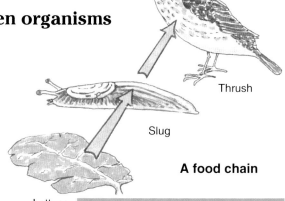

Thrush

Slug

A food chain

Lettuce

> Are omnivores secondary or tertiary consumers, or both?

Some plants live in soil which contains few nutrients. They need to improve their nutrition and do this by eating insects.

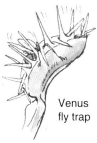

Sundew

Venus fly trap

> A vampire bat may suck some of a buffalo's blood without killing it. Is the buffalo the vampire bat's prey?

Carnivorous animals which need to kill other animals for food are called **predators**. The animals they eat are called their **prey**.

There are many types of predator, but only four general methods of catching prey:

Hunting is probably the most common predation method. The cheetah relies on its speed to **chase** and catch its prey.

Cheetah

Some animals **trap** their food. Beavers build dams partly in order to trap fish. However, the most well known predators which trap their prey are web-spinning spiders.

Orb web spider

Trap-door spiders also build a web, but they use it to hide behind before scurrying out to **ambush** passing food. All spiders are lone hunters.

Angler fish

Trap-door spider

A few animals **lure** their prey within reach of their mouths. The angler fish has a luminous blob on a stalk on its head. It waves this blob at smaller fish which think it is an even smaller fish. They chase this 'food' into the mouth of the angler fish.

> If a prey species evolves into a faster-running species, how might this affect the predators which chase them?

Many predators target weak or old prey because these are easier to catch than young, healthy organisms. This is an example of natural selection in action.

Are sickly prey animals more or less likely to pass on their genes than healthy ones?

How does this help the species as a whole?

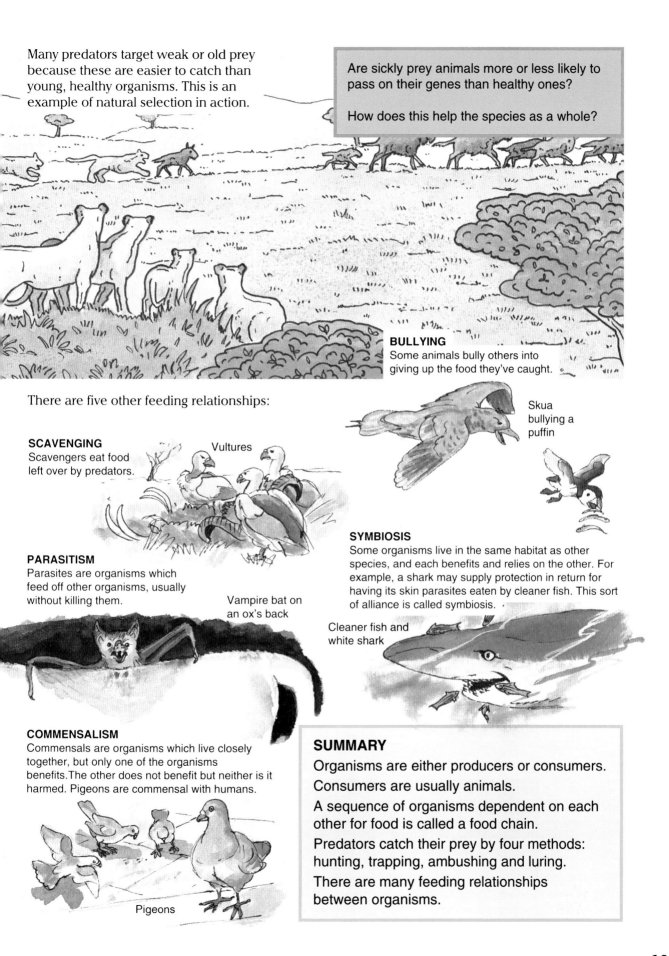

BULLYING
Some animals bully others into giving up the food they've caught.

Skua bullying a puffin

There are five other feeding relationships:

SCAVENGING
Scavengers eat food left over by predators.

Vultures

PARASITISM
Parasites are organisms which feed off other organisms, usually without killing them.

Vampire bat on an ox's back

SYMBIOSIS
Some organisms live in the same habitat as other species, and each benefits and relies on the other. For example, a shark may supply protection in return for having its skin parasites eaten by cleaner fish. This sort of alliance is called symbiosis.

Cleaner fish and white shark

COMMENSALISM
Commensals are organisms which live closely together, but only one of the organisms benefits. The other does not benefit but neither is it harmed. Pigeons are commensal with humans.

Pigeons

SUMMARY
Organisms are either producers or consumers.
Consumers are usually animals.
A sequence of organisms dependent on each other for food is called a food chain.
Predators catch their prey by four methods: hunting, trapping, ambushing and luring.
There are many feeding relationships between organisms.

THE BIOMASS

Food webs, chains and pyramids

Most feeding relationships between members of a community of organisms are more complicated than food chains. Instead they are called **food webs**. For example, a thrush may eat both snails and berries, and an omnivore might eat cabbages, berries, snails and thrushes.

A food web may be a small one within a single habitat, or it may be worldwide. Animals which travel, or **migrate** large distances take part in worldwide food webs:

A food web

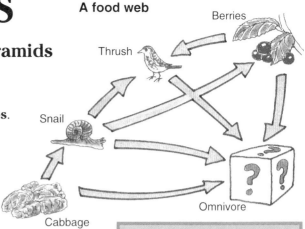

Thrush • Berries • Snail • Cabbage • Omnivore

What omnivore might eat all these organisms?

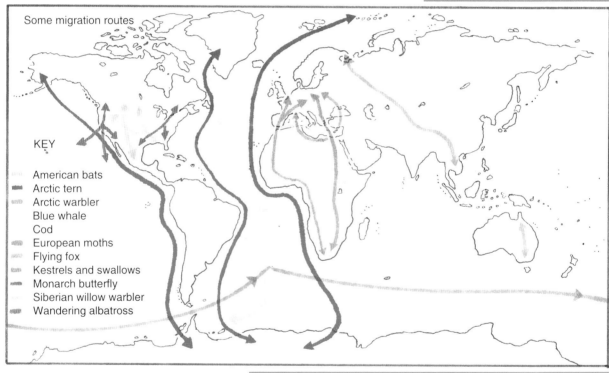

Some migration routes

KEY

- American bats
- Arctic tern
- Arctic warbler
- Blue whale
- Cod
- European moths
- Flying fox
- Kestrels and swallows
- Monarch butterfly
- Siberian willow warbler
- Wandering albatross

Investigation

Think of all the organisms you might find around your school. How might these organisms relate to each other and to neighbouring habitats and humans?

If you live inland, which common organism might connect local habitats with coastal habitats?

How do you think your local wildlife is connected to the worldwide food web?

All the Earth's organisms are interconnected, although the connections are not always obvious. All the organisms in the biosphere are called the Earth's **biomass**.

Sun

Rabbits

Grass

Rabbit droppings

Green plants grow by using between 3% and 12% of the sunlight energy which hits their surfaces.

A primary consumer, such as a rabbit or a snail, turns about 10% of the mass of its food into body material. In other words, it takes about 10 kg of grass to produce 1 kg of rabbit.

What do you think happens to the excreted material?

Energy in the form of radiated heat or movement energy is lost when food is converted into body material. Much of the food is turned into solid and liquid waste and is excreted. Secondary consumers only retain about 10% of the mass of their food. Tertiary consumers and further members of a food web or chain also only convert about 10% of their food into body material. The way body material decreases as it goes through a food chain can be shown as a **pyramid of biomass**.

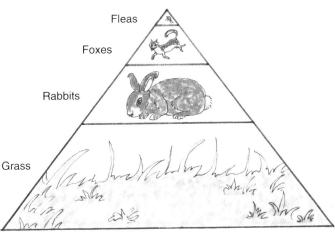

Fleas

Foxes

Rabbits

Grass

Pyramid of biomass

Fleas

Foxes

Rabbits

Grass

Pyramid of numbers

The number of organisms which can be supported on the upper levels of the pyramid is related to the numbers of organisms on the levels below. That means the pyramid of biomass can also be a **pyramid of numbers**.

Why do you think a large animal's parasites, such as fleas, are usually small and numerous?

SUMMARY
Food webs are complex feeding relationships.
All of the organisms on Earth make up the Earth's biomass.
The pyramid of biomass shows how total body material is lost at each stage of a food chain.
The pyramid of numbers shows the number of organisms that can be supported on each level of a pyramid of biomass.

DECAY

How decomposers relate to other organisms

When large organisms excrete, die, or lose parts of their bodies, some of their organic material is eaten by beetles and other scavengers. The rest is broken down, or decays, as the food chemicals are taken in by other organisms. These organisms, such as fungi and bacteria, are called **decomposers**. Decomposers make things rot. Most decomposers cannot produce their own food.

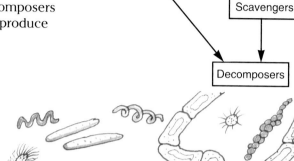

A teaspoon of damp, fertile soil may contain 12 billion bacteria and perhaps 300 metres of thin fungal threads

Magnified bacteria and fungal threads

As well as breaking down excreted material, decomposers also excrete their own wastes. These materials are nutrients for other decomposers and green plants. Two important chemicals in this waste material are carbon and nitrogen. These chemicals make up much of the cell matter of organisms. Because carbon and nitrogen goes round and round the biosphere, the processes involved are called the **carbon cycle** and the **nitrogen cycle**. Both cycles depend on the activities of decomposers.

Combined carbon and nitrogen cycles

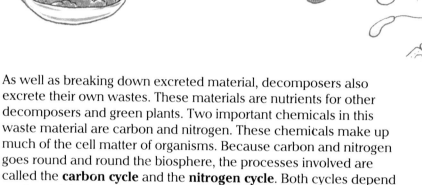

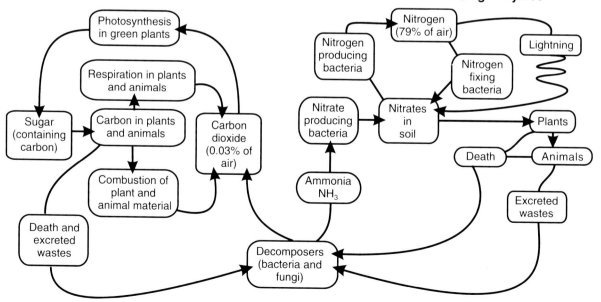

Most decomposers are single-celled organisms, such as fungi. Some types of fungus cells are able to join together to form large, visible communities, such as mushrooms. Most fungi live by breaking down dead organic material but some species are parasitic on plants and animals and a few behave like predators.

Do you think there are any decomposers inside your body?

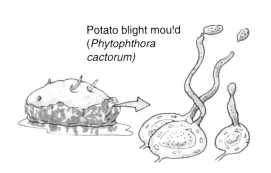

Potato blight mou!d (*Phytophthora cactorum*)

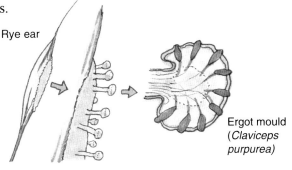

Rye ear

Ergot mould (*Claviceps purpurea*)

All animals carry bacteria around with them. Some are parasites and some are commensals. Many are stomach and intestine bacteria which help animals such as cows and termites to break down the tough plant food they eat. Humans have about 5 billion bacteria in their intestines, some of which have a symbiotic relationship with us. For example, the bacteria called *Escherichia coli* take some of our food and give us vitamin K in return. Humans need this vitamin to produce blood clotting agents.

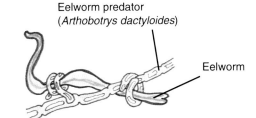

Eelworm predator (*Arthobotrys dactyloides*)

Eelworm

Some fungi

A type of fungus called *Arthobotrys dactyloides* can trap tiny soil creatures such as eelworms

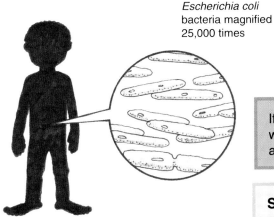

Escherichia coli bacteria magnified 25,000 times

Escherichia coli are helpful inside the intestine, but can eat skin if they get out. So as well as being symbiotic, what other feeding relationship can these species have with humans?

If all organic material except the decomposers were removed from the biosphere, do you think any decomposers would survive?

Many large organisms have special food needs. On the whole, decomposers can use a wider range of food material. This means that they are much more likely to survive a habitat catastrophe than large animals. The rest of the biomass depends on the decomposers, but the decomposers rely much less on larger living organisms for their survival.

SUMMARY

Organic material is broken down by organisms called decomposers.

Decomposers are vital parts of the carbon and nitrogen cycles.

Decomposers are small organisms such as fungi and bacteria.

Fungi and bacteria have a wide range of feeding relationships with other organisms.

USING MICROBES

How humans manage decomposing organisms

Tiny organisms which can only be seen through a microscope are called **microbes**. Humans use the activities of microbes for a wide range of purposes. One important use is the treatment of sewage. Untreated sewage contains excreted material, poisons, domestic chemicals and disease agents. These can all be cleaned up by the careful use of microbial activity.

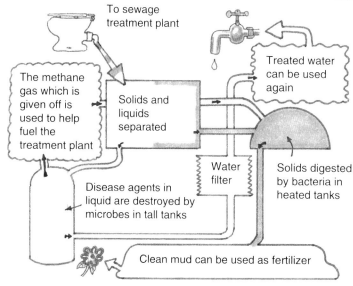

To sewage treatment plant

Treated water can be used again

The methane gas which is given off is used to help fuel the treatment plant

Solids and liquids separated

Water filter

Solids digested by bacteria in heated tanks

Disease agents in liquid are destroyed by microbes in tall tanks

Clean mud can be used as fertilizer

Why do you think untreated sewage should not be put straight on to farmland where soil microbes can decompose it?

Some sewage treatment microbes

Vorticella alba

Volvox

Euglypha

Spirillum

The decomposing activity of microbes is also used for making a number of foods and drinks.

Food	Bacteria	Fungi
Cheese	yes	yes
Yogurt	yes	no
Yeast extract	no	yes
Buttermilk	yes	no
Bread	no	yes
Beer	no	yes
Citric acid	yes	no

Which of these foods is produced by bacteria and which by fungi?

Some types of fungi produce poisons which kill bacteria. These poisons are called **antibiotics** and can be used as medicines to help cure bacterial infections.

The Scottish bacteriologist Alexander Fleming (1881–1955) discovered the antibiotic penicillin in 1928.

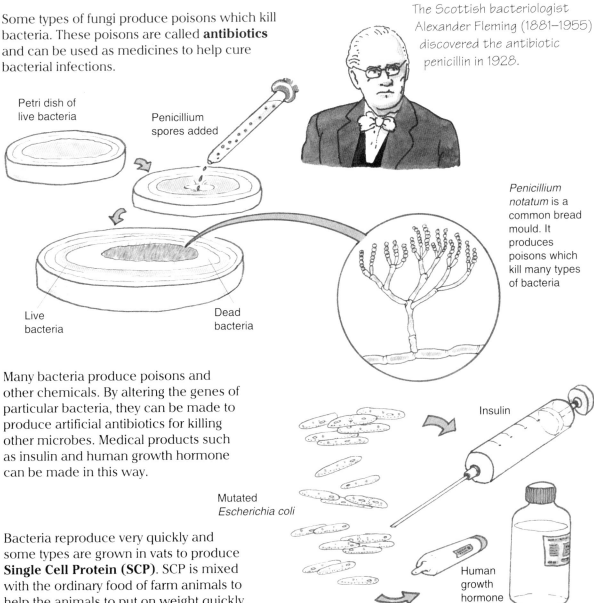

Petri dish of live bacteria

Penicillium spores added

Live bacteria

Dead bacteria

Penicillium notatum is a common bread mould. It produces poisons which kill many types of bacteria

Many bacteria produce poisons and other chemicals. By altering the genes of particular bacteria, they can be made to produce artificial antibiotics for killing other microbes. Medical products such as insulin and human growth hormone can be made in this way.

Mutated *Escherichia coli*

Insulin

Human growth hormone

Bacteria reproduce very quickly and some types are grown in vats to produce **Single Cell Protein (SCP)**. SCP is mixed with the ordinary food of farm animals to help the animals to put on weight quickly. Artificial antibiotics and yeast products may also be fed to animals.

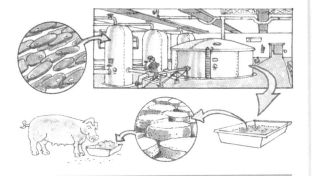

Why are farm animals given regular treatments of antibiotics?

SUMMARY

The activities of microbes are used by humans for the treatment of sewage.

Microbes are useful for the production of a wide range of foods and drinks.

Antibiotics are produced by some microbes and are used as medicines.

The genes of microbes can be changed so that they produce useful chemicals.

Bacteria can be grown in bulk quantities of Single Cell Protein which is used to feed farm animals.

MANAGING THE BIOMASS

How humans manage large organisms

As well as managing microbes, people have always managed or controlled large organisms. Before farming was developed, people were hunters of animals and gatherers of plants. Nowadays, the main human hunting activity is for sea food.

What other hunting activities can you think of?

Most people have no need to hunt for food, but go hunting and fishing as leisure activities. Special areas or times of the year are set aside for these things. This is to protect hunted species so that hunting can continue to be enjoyed. Animals hunted for sport are called **game**.

Some endangered species are protected by law, though illegal hunting of these animals still goes on. Game reserves are areas where endangered species can be protected from illegal hunting. Legal hunting is allowed in order to regulate populations. Killing wild animals to regulate the population is called **culling**. Some zoos also help to protect endangered species.

Some game animals

Mallard duck

Red deer

Sea trout

National parks and other areas may be set aside for the protection, or **conservation** of tree species. Other trees are grown for timber.

Why might some tree species be endangered?

Land usually needs to be cleared of existing vegetation before farming can take place. For example, about 5,000 years ago, Britain was almost completely covered by wild forests. Today, only about 8% of Britain is forested and 72% is farmland.

What do you think the other 20% of the area of Britain consists of?

3000BC   1300BC   AD 1995

Large, efficient farms help meet the food requirements of the world's human population. Sheep and cotton are farmed for **textile fibres**. A huge range of other products are grown for industrial, transport and construction purposes.

Australian sheep farm

Investigation
Think about the things in your kitchen. Which products came from forestry and which came from farming?

Spatula

Carrot

Bird's nest soup

Wine

Linen tea-towel

Chair

SUMMARY
Early humans were hunter-gatherers. Most food is now grown on farms.

Endangered species are protected in game reserves where only limited hunting is allowed.

Conservation areas help to protect endangered species.

Land is usually cleared of vegetation before farming can take place.

ARTIFICIAL HABITATS

Why humans create habitats

Clothes and houses can be thought of as artificial habitats. Clothes, farming and technology help humans to live anywhere on Earth. Naked humans can only survive if they live in a warm climate.

Humans also provide artificial habitats for other organisms. Some small modern farms grow crops and flowers in large troughs through which nutrients and water are pumped. This is called **hydroponic farming**. Other farms use huge greenhouses to help crops ripen earlier than usual and to grow crops which could not survive outside.

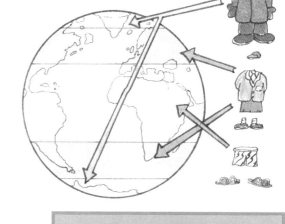

Where else can humans live if they take their habitat with them?

Hydroponic trough

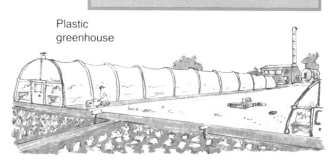

Plastic greenhouse

Houses and gardens comprise many artificial habitats. Many attractive garden plants would be unable to grow if garden soil was not managed properly. Decorative animals such as goldfish also benefit from some gardens.

Which organisms benefit from artificial habitats in this garden?

In Europe in the Middle Ages, monks kept ponds stocked with fish. This was because Christians were encouraged to eat fish on Fridays, so they needed to keep a ready supply. These days, fish such as salmon are often reared in artificial ponds at **fish farms**.

Fish farms are examples of **intensive farming**. More fish can be grown in a farm pool than can survive in a natural pool of the same size. Other modern farms practise the intensive farming of **livestock** such as cattle, pigs and poultry.

How do you think a salmon farm helps to protect wild salmon?

Some people think that livestock are happier and healthier indoors rather than out in a cold, damp field. What reasons can you give why this might not be so?

SUMMARY

Farming and technology allow the maintenance of artificial habitats.

Hydroponic troughs and greenhouses are examples of artificial habitats for plants.

Houses and gardens are artificial habitats for plants and animals.

Artificial habitats are built for intensive livestock farming.

PESTS, WEEDS AND DISEASES

How small organisms control humans

When many species of organism live in a habitat, it is said to have **biodiversity**. If conditions in the habitat do not much change, the number of each species does not much change. If there is biodiversity of plants in a habitat, there is likely to be a biodiversity of herbivores. When only one species of plant is grown in a large field, this is called **monoculture**.

A herbivore in a biodiverse habitat finds only a few of the plants it normally eats. When a herbivore finds a monoculture of its favourite food, it is suddenly surrounded by a feast. The herbivore population may then suddenly increase and the species becomes a **pest**.

Swarm of locusts

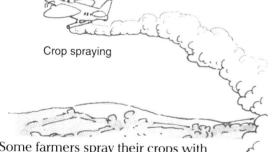

Crop spraying

If the natural predators of the herbivores are poisoned by chemicals, what will happen to the populations of the herbivores?

Some farmers spray their crops with poisons called **pesticides** which are designed to kill the pests. These may kill other wildlife and may make the crop poisonous. Instead of using one large field, some farmers spread their crops over a number of separate small fields to reduce the risk of pests. However, the soil in some of these fields may be less fertile than in others.

To grow more crops, some farmers use artificial **fertilizers** on the soil. Heavy use of fertilizers may destroy the decomposers which live in the soil.

Some fertilizers also encourage the growth of unwanted plants called weeds. Some farmers try to destroy weeds with weedkillers, or **herbicides**. Like pesticides and fertilizers, herbicides can also damage wildlife.

Some farmers use **biological weapons** to reduce pests and weeds. For example, in the 1950s, the rabbit disease myxomatosis was introduced into the rabbit population of Britain and Australia. This reduced the number of rabbits for a while. However, most wild rabbits are now adapted to this disease and have become **resistant** to it. The rabbit population has recovered. Some species of pests and weeds have become resistant to pesticides and herbicides.

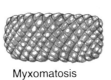

Myxomatosis microbe

Resistant weed

What other organisms on farms do you think might adapt to biological weapons?

The closer farm animals live to each other, the more likely they are to pass on infections. Intensively reared animals are likely to be infected, so they are given regular doses of antibiotics. Many disease organisms are now becoming resistant to these antibiotics. The number of new antibiotics which can be found is probably limited.

How resistance develops

Microbes

Most types of microbes are poisoned and die

Poison

A few mutated microbes resist the effects of the poison

Poison

The poison no longer works

Resistant microbes reproduce

Some farm animal diseases can be passed on to wild animals and humans. How do you think this will affect the populations of wild animals and humans?

A number of human disease organisms are developing resistance to antibiotics. For example, tuberculosis is a chest disease which was almost wiped out by antibiotics in many countries. Now a slightly altered form of tuberculosis is on the increase.

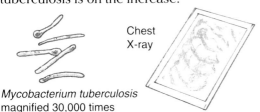

Chest X-ray

Mycobacterium tuberculosis magnified 30,000 times

SUMMARY

Biodiversity in a habitat helps to regulate the population of each species in the community.

Monocultures encourage attacks by pests.

Artificial pesticides, fertilizers and herbicides are used to improve crop production, but also damage wildlife.

Organisms can become resistant to pesticides, herbicides, diseases and antibiotics.

Key words appear in **bold** the first time
they occur in the text.

INDEX

First published in Great Britain by Heinemann Library,
an imprint of Heinemann Publishers (Oxford) Ltd,
Halley Court, Jordan Hill, Oxford, OX2 8EJ

MADRID   ATHENS   PARIS
FLORENCE   PRAGUE   WARSAW
PORTSMOUTH NH   CHACAGO   SAO PAULO
SINGAPORE   TOKYO   MELBOURNE   AUCKLAND
IBADAN   GABORONE   JOHANNESBURG

© Lazy Summer Books Ltd. 1995
First published 1995
99 98 97 96 95
10 9 8 7 6 5 4 3 2 1
British Library Cataloguing in Publication Data
is available on request from the British Library
ISBN   0–431–07608–1   (HB)
ISBN   0–431–07576–X   (PB)
Designed by Lazy Summer Books Ltd
Illustrated by Lazy Summer Books Ltd
Printed and bound in China